# OXFORD
## UNIVERSITY PRESS

# Big and Little

# Eli Francis

2 Look at this rhinoceros. It is big.

This parrot is little.

This elephant is big.

Now, look at this frog. It is little.

Look at this giraffe. It is big.

This butterfly is little.

# Picture Contrast Chart

**Big**

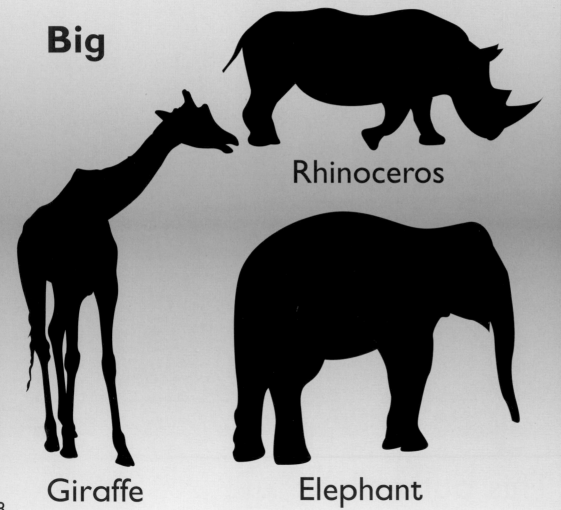

Rhinoceros

Giraffe

Elephant

**Little**

Parrot

Frog

Butterfly